Preface

The Sandhill Crane is one of North America's largest and oldest bird species, with some fossil records dating back almost 2.5 million years. Listening to them engage in cacophonous conversation, one can easily imagine an era when their songs filled the air with prehistoric splendor. They are tall, lanky birds but are graceful in flight. They form mating pairs for life. Both the male and female actively engage in brooding and raising of the young. Juvenile Sandhills remain with their parents and migrate as a family unit until the young become independent several weeks before the following nesting season. The young can be distinguished by the lack of a red forehead that is so characteristic of the adults.

One of the premiere locations for observing the wintering flocks is Bosque del Apache National Wildlife Refuge in San Antonio, New Mexico. The Sandhill Cranes in this book were photographed at Bosque del Apache over approximately 5 days spanning two seasons. A visit to see these magnificent creatures is time well spent!

I hope you enjoy reading this book with your children and take the time to see what a Sandhill sees!

Dr DAD Books is a trademark of Children's Wildlife Books by Daniel A. D'Auria MD

ISBN 10/ISBN13 1470168073/978-1470168070

A Sandhill Sees

Written and Photographed
by
Daniel A. D'Auria MD

I see you there...

You're watching me.

It's Sandhill Cranes you've come to see.

You're in the place that you should be!

A refuge called Bosque del Apache.

It's south we go when weather chills.

We flap our wings and point our bills.

A long, long distance we do fly...

One thousand miles or more up high!

If you watch us I would bet...

the things you'll see you won't regret.

We stand in water for the night...

to keep away the things that bite!

But in the morning light you'll see...

We fly out to the fields. We're free!

At times you'll note we jump about,

But just until we figure out...

Just whose spot is here or there.

Sometimes we're jumping everywhere!

We jump for show....

We jump for poise...

We jump for thrills.....

We jump for joy!

And if you hang around I fear...

A lot of noisy sounds you'll hear!

At times you'll see our heads held low.

We're telling you it's time to go!

We dip our heads and stretch our necks...

And off we go on skyward treks.

We hang around while weather's cool...

and food's - a - plenty. That's the rule!

When the season's come to pass,

We'll fly up north, until at last...

Winter's gone, the sun is bright,

And longer days bring shorter nights.

You see me here....
I'm watching you!

You watch with eyes and cameras too.

A human being I've come to find.

I wonder......

does that cross your mind?

Enjoy the growing library
of titles by DrDAD
All available at
www.DrDADBooks.com

Made in the USA
Monee, IL
07 July 2026

56551351R00026